ACTION GUIDE

unshockable love

how Jesus changes the world through imperfect people

John Burke

Action Guide v. 1.1

Written by Craig L. Whitney and John Burke

Copyright © 2013 Gateway Leadership Initiative

All rights reserved. Written permission must be secured from the publisher to reproduce any part of this book, except for brief quotations in critical reviews or articles.

Scriptures taken from the Holy Bible, New International Version®, NIV®. Copyright © 1973, 1978, 1984, 2011 by Biblica, Inc.™ Used by permission of Zondervan. All rights reserved worldwide. www.zondervan.com The "NIV" and "New International Version" are trademarks registered in the United States Patent and Trademark Office by Biblica, Inc.™

How To Use This Action Guide

Thanks so much for purchasing this Action Guide for my book, *Unshockable Love*. I hope you and your small group or leadership team will find your exploration of the book as challenging and meaningful as I did in creating it. As you'll see in the book, I'm definitely passionate about the timeliness and importance of this message for Christ followers everywhere. Yet, I know I'm just one member of Christ's Body. My voice alone simply can't bring about the kind of large-scale change I truly believe Jesus longs to see happen in churches all across the country and the world. I know that whatever real change is going to happen is going to start with you. It's through small groups of devoted Christ followers just like you–people willing to take an honest look at themselves and take bold steps to follow Jesus in a more transparent, grace-filled way–that real change will come. That's why I want you to know I'm praying for you...that God will grant you grace to grow in the attitude and actions of Jesus.

We've created this Action Guide because it's not enough to *know* about Jesus' attitude and actions, we want to actually *do* the things that will help us be more and more like Jesus to the world around us. That's what this Action Guide is designed to do. Think of the Action Guide as a companion to use over the course of a year with whatever curriculum you are using after *Unshockable Love*. The goal is not to "finish" in a certain period of time, but to work new habits and behaviors of engagement into your life and the life of your group in order to help you begin the formation of a Network to *be* His Body to your world.

Here's how it works. The Action Guide is designed so that each person can work on different exercises each week, and occasionally your whole group will have exercises you can do together. Take 10 to 15 minutes each time your group meets to check in:

1. Assess – What attitudes or actions did you work on since your last meeting and how did it go?

2. Next – What's your (or our) next exercise to try?

Finally, I'd love to hear from you! Share with us your thoughts and impressions from your exploration of *Unshockable Love* and let us know how this Action Guide has impacted your small group or leadership team. For ongoing thoughts, resources, and coaching to help you live on mission with Jesus and each other, check out www.UnshockableLove.com.

God's blessings,

How To Find The Right Exercise Routine

Developing the attitudes and actions of Jesus is a lot like getting in shape. You will need to develop new ways of thinking and doing over time. Think of this Action Guide as your fitness plan. Each exercise will help you develop the attitudes and actions of Jesus in your own life and the life of your group. Some of them you can do once to help you assess where you are or plan your next steps. Others will need to be done consistently in order to build new habits and relationships. We've organized them to help you get started and stay at it. Core activities are exercises essential to become like Jesus and creating a wave of impact on those around you. Extra activities are designed to help you assess, plan or get unstuck, so use them as needed.

Warm-ups: Attitude Adjustment

These exercises will challenge you to begin engaging people with attitudes and actions of Jesus.

CORE	EXTRAS
Seeing Past the Mud 3	
Unshockable 5	
Be Available 7	
Call Out the Masterpiece 9	

Core, Context, Clarity:

These exercises will help you start a group or focus your current group to create a wave of impact.

CORE	EXTRAS
Invite Others 11	Know Your Gifts 17
Prayer Walk 13	Make a Covenant 19
Seeing Needs 15	Draw A Map 21

Building Relational Momentum:

These exercises will help you and your group build relational momentum with those who are not following Jesus.

CORE	EXTRAS
Pray 4:4 23	Check Your Connections 35
Walk Don't Wave 25	Make Room 37
Have Fun with a Purpose 27	Create a Rhythm 39
Make a Meal that Matters 29	
Throw a Party 31	
Start a Group 33	

Serve Your Neighbors With Your Neighbors:
These exercises will help you begin meeting physical and spiritual needs around you.

CORE	EXTRAS
Serve Someone 41	Go to the Hurting 47
Throw a Serve Party 43	Heart Storming 49
Find A Cause to Serve 45	

"Come as you are" Spiritual Conversations:
These exercises will help you invite those who aren't following Jesus into spiritual conversations and environments.

CORE	EXTRAS
Start Spiritual Conversations 51	Have Powerful Conversations 61
Listen for Their Spiritual Story 53	Speak the Truth in Love 63
Telling Your Spiritual Story 55	
Share the Good News 57	
A "Come as You Are" Invitation 59	

Everyone Can Develop Someone:
These exercises will help you develop those who come to faith into followers of Jesus.

CORE	EXTRAS
Point the Way 65	Know How You Grow 71
Find a Running Partner 67	Index 73
Growing Deep 69	

ACTION GUIDE

unshockable love

how Jesus changes the world
through imperfect people

John Burke

Seeing Past the Mud

When the Pharisees saw this, they asked his disciples, "Why does your teacher eat with tax collectors and 'sinners'?" On hearing this, Jesus said, "It is not the healthy who need a doctor, but the sick. But go and learn what this means: 'I desire mercy, not sacrifice.' For I have not come to call the righteous, but sinners."
~ Matthew 9:11-13

This exercise is based on the "Try This" activity in Chapter 1 on p. 36 in *Unshockable Love*.

> Jesus was a friend of sinners. He saw in them the identity God created them to live out. Our problem is too often we see what they are right now–the mud instead of the Masterpiece. To demonstrate the unshockable love of Jesus we need a new way of seeing others. The goal of this exercise is to intentionally open your heart to those you see as muddied, and to learn their story in order to discover the Masterpiece God wants to restore. If you're a natural conversationalist, you may find this easy. If you're not, you can still have great conversations, you'll just need to stretch yourself. The Holy Spirit will give you the ability and courage if you are willing.

How

Your days are filled with many opportunities to interact with people. These simple steps, done consistently and intentionally, will help you develop a more Jesus-like heart and vision.

- **Start with prayer.**

    Begin each day asking God to help you see people the way he does. Ask him to show you someone during your day that you could interact with. Tell God in advance that you're willing to respond when the Holy Spirit prompts you.

- **Be ready for opportunities.**

    You might start a conversation with someone at work, a person at the store or in your neighborhood. Approach your day with your head up, your eyes open, and your heart ready to see someone you could interact with.

- **Ask questions.**

    Just be curious. It's not an investigation or interrogation. You're just hoping to learn a little about them – maybe where they are from, what they do, or what they like.

- **Look for the Masterpiece**

    This is where your attitude adjustment takes place. As you converse, ask God to show you his artistry.

Act
For the next week, I will try to intentionally interact with at least one person each day, looking for the work of the Master in them. (Write down their names and what you learned about them).

Assess
- What did you find most difficult about this exercise?
- Who was the most interesting person you met?
- How has this experience helped you see others with the eyes of Jesus?

Next (suggested exercises)
Be Available
Call out the Masterpiece
Go to the Hurting
Walk Don't Wave

Unshockable

*Therefore, I tell you, her many sins have been forgiven--for she loved much.
But he who has been forgiven little loves little.*
~ Luke 7:47

This exercise is based on the "Try This" activity in Chapter 2 on p. 50 in *Unshockable Love*.

> Nothing shocked Jesus. That's not to say he was without feeling. He had great compassion for those who were hurting (Matt. 9:36). He grieved with those who were grieving (John 11:35). But he was never shocked by sin because he knew it was the result of broken relationship. Instead of condemnation, Jesus offered relationship–it was his solution for sin.
>
> We are often shocked by the things people do. We hear about horrible evils on the news. We see people doing things that hurt others and themselves. We hear people brag about their own sinful behavior. As people who love Jesus and his ways, we are shocked. When we feel that way we need to remember they are just like us, imperfect people loved by the God of grace who created them. Our debts cost God the same as their debts.
>
> The goal of this exercise is to put that attitude into action–to interact with those who make us uncomfortable because something in their lives is shocking to us. It may be their past, their pain, or their perspective. Are you willing to offer restorative relationship? That's what it takes to be like Jesus!

How

If you normally avoid things that make you uncomfortable, this exercise will challenge you to do the opposite–to move toward people you would normally avoid. These simple steps will help you do so with the same attitude as Jesus.

- **Start with prayer.**

    Begin each day confessing your sin and thanking God for his forgiveness. Read Luke 18:9-14, asking God to help you see yourself and others the way he does. Then ask him to show you someone during your day that you are shocked by or uncomfortable with. Tell God in advance that you're willing to respond when the Holy Spirit prompts you.

- **Consider who comes to mind.**

    As you pray, certain people may come to mind. It might be someone at work or a homeless person you pass on the way there. Pay attention to the promptings; they may be the very people God wants you to interact with.

- **Ask questions.**

  Approach them with an open heart. Ask questions. Be curious. You don't need to ask about the thing that makes you uncomfortable. Start a conversation like you would with anyone you wanted to know better.

- **Communicate value.**

  As you learn about people, look for something worth praising. Tell them what you appreciate about who they are or what they are doing.

Act

This week, I will push out of my comfort zone to interact with as many people as I can who might make me uncomfortable. (Write down each person you interact with and what you learn about the person).

Assess
- What did you find most difficult about this exercise?
- What was the most surprising thing you learned about someone you talked with?
- How has this experience helped you see others with the eyes of Jesus?

Next (suggested exercises)
Call out the Masterpiece
Start Spiritual Conversations
Go to the Hurting

Be Available

Not everyone who says to me, 'Lord, Lord,' will enter the kingdom of heaven, but only he who does the will of my Father who is in heaven.
~ Matthew 7:21

This exercise is based on the "Try This" activity on p. 70 in *Unshockable Love*.

> Jesus' whole life was oriented towards doing the will of his father. From his first visit to the temple in Jerusalem (Luke 2:49), to his long night in the garden (Matt. 26:39), he was always available to do his father's will.
>
> A lack of availability is often what keeps us from being like Jesus. Life is busy, hectic, packed full of stuff to do from early in the morning until late at night. It's not that you don't want to do God's will, there just isn't time. What would happen if you planned in advance to put what God wants ahead of whatever you have planned?
>
> The goal of this exercise is simply to give God and others priority in your day. By being decisive and responsive you will see what God can do through you to restore value in others.

How

The most important part of this exercise is deciding to be available to whomever God wants you to love and serve. These tips will help:

- **Make a commitment.**

  There is a difference between saying "I might" and "I will." This exercise starts by saying "I will." Start by telling God in prayer, "I will be available to whomever you show me today." Tell your group or running partners, "I will be available to whomever God shows me this week." When an opportunity comes and you think you don't have time, remember your commitment.

- **Create a reminder.**

  Busyness propels us like a moving sidewalk. Before you know it your day is over and the commitment you made in the morning is both forgotten and undone. Create a reminder for yourself–an alarm on your watch every hour, a note packed with your lunch, an app on your phone–that brings to mind your commitment.

The *Soul Revolution* app is free at Android and iPhone app stores to remind you every hour to respond to God's promptings.

- **See it and say it.**
  When you see an opportunity to encourage someone or restore value, say it. Call out a positive, God-given trait you see: "You're a great parent." "You're a hard worker." "That's so cool how you volunteer." Push through your worries of coming off "insincere"—it feels awkward because we're not used to encouraging people. If you're unsure, ask, "Lord, is this opportunity from you?" Then give his will priority.

Act

This week, I will be available to encourage and restore value to others when God shows me the opportunity. (Write down the names of people you encouraged or demonstrated value toward and chronicle what you did and how you felt afterward).

Assess
- What did you find most difficult about this exercise?
- Did you miss any opportunities because you were too busy? Were you available for opportunities you might have missed in the past?
- What would it be like to be available every day?

Next (suggested exercises)

Call Out the Masterpiece
Start Spiritual Conversations
Go to the Hurting
Walk Don't Wave

Calling out the Masterpiece

*Jesus reached out his hand and touched the man. "I am willing," he said. "Be clean!"
And immediately the leprosy left him.*
~ Luke 5:13

This exercise is based on the "Try This" activity in Chapter 4 on p. 88 in *Unshockable Love*.

> Jesus called out the Masterpiece in the most unlikely of people–even a leper. Imagine living an isolated life, segregated from family and friends because of a disease that made you untouchable and "unclean." Then imagine someone willing to reach out his hand and touch you. How much value would that single touch restore to your de-valued soul?
>
> Most of us will never meet a person with leprosy. However, every day we pass by people who feel like lepers–isolated, alone, and untouchable. What if you could be the person to call out the Masterpiece in them to say, "You have value and here's why?"
>
> The goal of this exercise is simply to practice calling out the Masterpiece. It doesn't matter who, when, where, or why–just see value in people and tell them.

How

Speaking encouraging words is difficult—we're conditioned to see what's wrong, what's missing, and often we're just too busy to stop and consider how to speak encouraging words. Here are a few ideas to help you see and call out the Masterpiece in others:

- **Stop.**

    Create reminders in your day to stop for one minute. That's all it takes to be an encourager.

- **Look.**

    Look at who's around you and what they are doing. Ask, "Lord, whom could I encourage right now? What do you see and want said?"

- **Speak.**

    Go to that person and say something encouraging. You don't need to make a speech, just be positive and affirming. You could point out something about the kind of person they are–"I really appreciate your focus." You could thank them for something they've done–"Thanks for helping with that project." It could be as simple as, "You know, I'm really glad we're neighbors."

Act
This week, I will try to say encouraging words, and convey value, to at least three people. (Write down who you encouraged and what you said or did to call out the Masterpiece).

Assess
- What kind of reactions did you get to your words of encouragement?
- How would it change you to become a person who constantly called out the Masterpiece in others?

Next (suggested exercises)
Go to the Hurting
Share the Good News
Walk Don't Wave

Invite Others

*After this the Lord appointed seventy-two others and sent them two by two
ahead of him to every town and place where he was about to go.*
~ Luke 10:1

If you've gotten this far, you've probably taken to heart that Jesus wants you to reflect his attitudes and actions to your family, friends and neighbors. You're also likely to feel overwhelmed. Where do you start? What should you do? How will you get it done? We'd suggest you start by inviting others to join you.

Consider this: Jesus never sent anyone out on mission by themselves. When he sent out the twelve disciples, he sent them two by two (Mark 6:7). When he sent out the 70, he sent them two by two (Luke 10:1). When the Holy Spirit sent messengers from the church in Antioch to share the Good News with other cities throughout the Roman Empire, he sent them out two by two, and Paul and Barnabas took along John Mark for extra help (Acts 13:2). Yes, Jesus wants you to be a messenger of his grace to your Network, but he doesn't want you to do it alone. This exercise will help you find others to share these experiences with and hopefully together form the core of a new Network of Christ followers, restoring the world around them by re-presenting Him.

How

Finding others to join you on this adventure of becoming like Jesus shouldn't be complicated, but it will require courage, initiative, and follow-through to get the journey started. If you already have a small group, discuss this exercise with each other. Use this to clarify what you're committing to do together.

- **Start with prayer**

  Before Jesus chose his twelve disciples, he spent a whole night in prayer. His example is an important one to follow, because inviting others into mission is one of the most important things we do. Here are a few practical ways to do this:

  - Start by telling God what's on your heart. Express what it is you believe he wants you to do.

  - You may already have some people in mind. Write their names down. Then, ask God to bring to your mind individuals he would want you to invite into this adventure. Add their names to your list.

  - Spend several days praying for the people you've listed. Ask God to prepare them to hear your heart and invitation.

- **Have a plan**

  Sharing a vague idea makes it easy for people to be excited, but inactive. Sharing an idea with a plan invites people to be part of making it happen. Here are a few suggestions:

  - If you are able, give people a copy of *Unshockable Love* to read. Your willingness to give them a copy speaks volumes about your excitement for what you've read.

  - Set a time and place and invite them to join you in discussing the book. We've created a six-session Discussion Guide to guide your conversations (available on Amazon).

  - You can use the exercises in this Action Guide as part of your discussion and/or to continue your action plan when the six weeks are over.

- **Make the ask**

  This is where courage comes in. It will help to remember that you aren't just asking people to join you; you're inviting them to join Jesus in what he wants to do in and through them. Follow these steps to make your invitation appealing:

  - Tell a story–preferably an exciting one.
    Is there some event or experience that God used to grab your heart and compel you to be all in? That story is the "why." Telling it well connects other people's hearts to your heart and together to God's heart.

  - Paint a picture–preferably an inviting one.
    There is a real future God has put on your heart. That picture is the "where." Painting it well makes people want to go there with you.

  - Describe the steps–preferably simple ones.
    There is a way to get from where you are to where God is calling you to go. Those steps are the "how." Describing them clearly gives people steps to take.

  - Make the ask–preferably a clear one.
    There is something you want them to say "yes" to, and this is the "what." Asking boldly invites people to say "YES" with confidence.

Act

In the next _____ days, I will invite _____ people to join me in exploring how we can restore the world around us by demonstrating the attitudes and actions Jesus.

Assess

- Were any of the people God brought to mind a surprise to you?
- How did you feel about asking? About the way people responded?
- How will your journey be different because you invited others to join you?

Next (suggested exercises)

Make a Covenant
Make Room
Start a Group

Prayer Walk

*And pray in the Spirit on all occasions with all kinds of prayers and requests.
With this in mind, be alert and always keep on praying for all the saints.*
~ Ephesians 6:18

> Prayer is powerful. Jesus set an example by praying regularly, often for long periods of time. As his representatives, one of the most powerful things we can do for others is simply pray for them. Prayer walking is a simple and effective way to do that.
>
> You can certainly pray for the people around you without walking, but walking will open your eyes to specific ways to pray that you would never see without going on a prayer walk.
>
> A prayer walk, then, has a dual purpose. It is an opportunity for God to show you what he sees in the places where you live. It is also an opportunity for you to share with God the people and places you care about.

How

A prayer walk doesn't need to be complicated. In fact it can be as simple as walking and praying. Here are some tips to make the most of your time as you get started:

- **Plan your walk.**

    Decide in advance when and where you will walk and how far or how long. It may be around your neighborhood, around your place of work, or among a certain group of people. Knowing these things in advance will help you focus on praying while walking.

- **Pray with your eyes open.**

    There are obvious reasons for this, but the most important is to see the people and needs around you. Start by asking God to help you see with his eyes. As you see people and things, let what you see shape your prayer.

- **Be normal**

    Keep in mind what Jesus said about the Pharisee praying in the temple (Luke 18:9-14). Calling attention to yourself, or your praying, is not the point of a prayer walk. If you're walking alone, you can pray silently and look like any other person out for a walk. If you're walking together, pray conversationally like friends enjoying a walk together.

- **Be friendly**

    If you meet others on your walk, greet them. Don't see them as interruptions but instead opportunities to meet someone new and learn more about the people and place where you are prayer walking.

Act
In the next _____ (time), I/we will walk _____ (where) in order to pray for those who live or work there.

Assess
- What did you see on your prayer walk that you didn't expect to see?
- Did prayer walking change what you think or feel about the people you prayed for?
- How would regular prayer walking change your ability to restore the people around you?

Next (suggested exercises)
Seeing Needs
Pray 4:4
Find a Cause to Serve

Seeing Needs

When he saw the crowds, he had compassion on them, because they were harassed and helpless, like sheep without a shepherd.
~ Matthew 9:36

Reading the Gospels, you will see it over and over again. Jesus was moved by compassion when he saw the needs of the people around him. He had compassion on the sick (Matt. 14:14), the blind (Matt. 20:34), the lepers (Mark 1:41), and the hungry (Mark 8:2). To be like Jesus is to be a person who sees, feels, and meets the needs of those around you – but it all starts with seeing.

The problem is that contemporary life is not made for seeing. Take a look at your calendar—it tells the story well. Most days, the world around you is just a blur of busyness...until you focus on what God sees. Suddenly, needs are everywhere. A woman with a toddler beside a busy street. Huge housing complexes littered with trash. A small boy pushed in a playground; another waiting alone on the steps of his school late in the afternoon. The needs are right in front of you; you just need to open your eyes to see them.

The goal is to become a person who lives with eyes open; a person able and willing to see the needs Jesus sees, and be like Jesus to someone else.

How

We see what we are looking for, so for the next week at the least, proactively look for needs. When you see one, make a note of it. There's no rule on how many needs you should find, but—if you're looking—this could be an almost constant practice. These tips will help you get started.

- **Use the same system to record each need you see.**

  Creating a routine will not only help you record what you see, but it will also help you develop the habit of looking. You could:

  - Carry a journal or small notebook.
  - Send yourself a text, reminder, email, or phone message.

- **Look for all kinds of needs.**

  Don't limit your eyes, or your heart. Look for all kinds of needs in all kinds of people. The child walking alone may need a friend as much as the single mom needs a babysitter. The guy drinking alone may need a purpose as much as the homeless man is needing a meal. Look for needs that are:

  - Financial
  - Physical
  - Social
  - Spiritual

- **Keep it simple.**

    You don't need to write or record a novel. Just note the basic facts like a journalist would.

    - Who (don't need a name, just man, woman, child…)
    - What (what do they need)
    - Where (where did you see them)

Act
For the next _____ (time) I will keep a record of every need I see during the course of my daily routine.

Assess
- How did paying attention change what you saw?
- Which needs surprised you? Which were the most heartbreaking?
- How would looking for needs every day change your attitudes and actions?

Next (suggested exercises)
Draw a Map
Walk Don't Wave
Serve Someone
Find a Cause to Serve

Know Your Gifts

We have different gifts, according to the grace given us. If a man's gift is prophesying, let him use it in proportion to his faith. If it is serving, let him serve; if it is teaching, let him teach; if it is encouraging, let him encourage; if it is contributing to the needs of others, let him give generously; if it is leadership, let him govern diligently; if it is showing mercy, let him do it cheerfully.
~ Romans 12:6-8

As you go on mission with Jesus and each other, it will be extremely helpful to know each other's unique Passions, Experiences, and Gifts. P.E.G. each other, because this will help you connect new people to those with common interests. This will also help you know who will be good at planning the party and who will be best at inviting lots of people to come. So take the time as you begin this journey together to know your Passions, Experiences, and Gifts.

If everyone were good at everything we wouldn't need each other. That isn't the way God made us. The Bible is very clear that together we make a body and each of us needs others to be complete (2 Cor. 12). This is especially true if we are going to re-present Jesus to those around us, because it is only together that we can fully re-present his body to the world.

All of us can probably articulate what we're passionate about—what gets us excited, or stirs us to want to act? Our experiences (good and bad) are also valuable because they are our touch point with humanity—what we share in common with others. Unfortunately, many people don't know what their spiritual gifts are. Others may be fearful because they've seen spiritual gifts used in ways that make them uncomfortable. These gifts are simply a special ability the Holy Spirit has given each of us to love and serve others in order to build up the body of Christ.

How

Here are some simple steps you can take individually or as a group to P.E.G. yourself:

- **List your passions.**

  Brainstorm and write down some of things that stir your passion. Maybe you're passionate about helping struggling kids, or single moms or dads, because you've been there. Maybe you're passionate about shopping, football, mountain-biking, or dancing (God can use all of these). Maybe you're passionate about telling others about God's heart for them. Whatever stirs you or gets you excited, write it down.

- **Reflect on your experiences.**

  Brainstorm and write down the formative experiences (positive and negative) in your life.

- **Discover your gifts.**

  Spiritual gifts are one of those issues where people often say, "If God would just tell me what my gifts are I would use them!" He may not have tattooed them on your forehead, but he has definitely left some clues, and these steps will help:

  - Ask your friends. Other people are often better at seeing what we are good at than we are. Start by asking your group or other Christ followers you have close relationships with about your spiritual gifts. Here's a great question, "What am I most likely doing when you see God working through me?"

  - Take a spiritual gifts test. There are many different types. None of them are perfect, yet each of them can help you in the discovery process. Here are links to a few we would recommend:

    http://gifts.churchgrowth.org/cgi-cg/gifts.cgi?intro=1

    http://buildingchurch.net/g2s.htm

  - Practice. Think about it, even the most gifted athlete goes into training. Musical prodigies still practice. The gifts God has given you will never be fully developed if you don't practice using them.

Act

P.E.G. yourself this week. Then take time to share your Passions, Experiences, and Gifts with those in your group, or those you're partnering with in this endeavor. Discuss how knowing each other's P.E.G. can help you work together as Christ's body on mission together.

Assess

- Were you surprised by what others said your gifts were? The test(s)?
- How would developing your gifts help you be more effective on mission with Jesus and others?

Next (suggested exercises)

Seeing Needs
Heart Storming
Find a Cause to Serve

Make a Covenant

*They devoted themselves to the apostles' teaching and to the fellowship,
to the breaking of bread and to prayer.*
~ Acts 2:42

As you begin to meet with a few friends and explore what it means to go on mission with Jesus, it will be helpful to create a group covenant – shared agreements about how your group will function. A covenant is the way God relates to us. In the Old Testament he created a covenant with Noah (Gen. 6), Abraham (Gen. 12:1-3), and David (2 Sam. 7:12-13). Jesus created a new covenant with us, his followers (Luke 22:19-20). The early church created a similar kind of covenant relationship with each other (Acts 2:42). By creating a group covenant of shared agreements, everyone will know what he or she is committing to.

How

In the time of the Old Testament, covenants were often sealed with blood (Gen. 15). That may seem a bit extreme to your group members, so here are a few helpful tips for creating a covenant:

- **Put it in writing.**

    The simple act of writing it down formalizes your agreement, but that doesn't mean it needs to sound like a contract. In fact one of the big differences between a covenant and a contract is that a covenant is about how we will help each other, while a contract is about how we will protect ourselves from each other. (See the "shared agreements" in Session 1 of the *Unshockable Love Discussion Guide* for an example.)

- **Get everyone on board.**

    The covenant is each person's promise of what he or she will do as part of the group, so it's important to make sure everyone agrees with everything that's in the covenant. Two simple questions will help. First, ask, "Are you clear about what is expected of you?" Next, ask, "Do you agree to do it?" Make adjustments until everyone is on board.

- **Have a ceremony.**

    It might sound awkward or cheesy to have a ceremony, but even simple celebrations are powerful. You can do it simply by having each person sign the covenant and then pray together for strength to keep it, or you can sign it and throw a party. Whether you go big or small, do something that makes the covenant official.

Act
As a group, we will write and agree to a covenant of shared agreements at our next meeting.

Assess
- How did you feel about creating and committing to a covenant?
- How do you believe your experience as a group will be different because you did?

Next (suggested exercises)
Know Your Gifts
Make Room
Start a Group
Create a Rhythm

Draw a Map

But you will receive power when the Holy Spirit comes on you; and you will be my witnesses in Jerusalem, and in all Judea and Samaria, and to the ends of the earth.
~ Acts 1:8

> Have you ever noticed that "place" has a prominent role in the Bible? God promised Abraham a place. Jesus was born in a place. The Good News about him spread from place to place as people took the message with them. And, God has put you in a place–a place he wants to restore.
>
> As you begin going on mission with Jesus, it may be helpful for you and your Network to think about your place. Where is it God has collectively placed you? What about this place, and the people who live and work here, is unique? How will you best be able to re-present Jesus to them?
>
> The goal of this exercise is to help your group or Network develop a clear focus–a people and place that God has called you to serve and help restore.

How

These instructions are based on Google maps. You could do the same thing with a printed map.

1. **Create a map at http://maps.google.com/.**
    a. Click on "My Places"
    b. You will need to sign in or create a Google account
    c. Click on "Create A Map"
    d. Save it as "My Network"

2. **Add the people in your Network.**
    a. For each person that is part of your Network, search for his or her home address and save it to the map. (Google will put a pin on their address.)
    b. Use the pin tool to add other key locations, such as places of work, schools that children attend, or other locations that members of your Network visit often.

3. **Draw a boundary.**
    a. Zoom out so you can see the people and places on your map.
    b. Use the line tool to draw a boundary around the geography your Network will focus on.
    c. Keep in mind you are not excluding people outside the boundary from your Network, you are just clarifying the focus of whom your Network will include.

Once you have drawn your map, you can share the link with others in your Network or capture an image and place it in a document. You may end up with one place or several places your Network will agree to focus on.

Act
I/we will focus our energy on restoring the people and place in _____ (place) as described in our map.

Assess
- How did you feel about drawing a map to focus your mission?
- Were you tempted to make the map too big? Or too small?
- How will having a map help your group or Network focus its energy?

Next (suggested exercises)
Prayer Walk
Find a Cause to Serve
Throw a Serve Party

Pray 4:4

I urge, then, first of all, that requests, prayers, intercession and thanksgiving be made for everyone-- for kings and all those in authority, that we may live peaceful and quiet lives in all godliness and holiness. This is good, and pleases God our Savior, who wants all men to be saved and to come to a knowledge of the truth. ~ 1Timothy 2:1-4

Jesus prayed–a lot. He would get up early in the morning and leave the house by himself to pray (Mark 1:35). He would spend all night in prayer (Luke 6:12). Jesus knew that prayer was essential if he was to accomplish what he came to do. Our own ability to re-present the attitudes and actions of Jesus will also be dependent on constant prayer.

The goal of this exercise is to begin praying specifically for four people you know to come to know and follow Jesus. You probably know a lot more than four people, and you may feel compelled to pray for all of them–that's a good thing. Specifically praying for four people you want to see come to faith will do at least two things. First, it will keep you focused. When you make the commitment to pray for certain people daily you will naturally pay more attention to what's happening in their lives. Second, and more importantly, you will invite God's power and presence into those relationships. He is able to give you wisdom to know what to do or say and the courage to do it. The Holy Spirit is also working in the other people's lives to show them God's goodness and draw them into a relationship with Jesus. Remember, God wants the people you are praying for to live in relationship with him even more than you do.

How

Praying for others is not difficult, but doing it consistently will require discipline and intentionality. Here are some tips to help:

- **Set aside a time and place to pray.**

  You might get up a few minutes early and go to your favorite chair. You could use your drive time to or from work. Praying consistently at the same time and place will soon become a habit.

- **Create reminders to pray during the day.**

  If you see the people often, pray for them every time you see them. Put reminders in your calendar or phone. These simple reminders can help you stay in an attitude of prayer all day.

- **Pray for their needs.**

  If you have relationships with them, ask them how you can pray for them. If they, or someone in their family is sick, pray for healing. If they have financial needs, pray for provision. If they are struggling in a relationship, pray for love and peace. Each of these needs is an opportunity for them to see God at work in their lives.

- **Pray for willingness.**

    Some on your list might already be curious about Jesus. Others may be very skeptical or even antagonistic toward him. Regardless of where they are now, pray that they would become willing to hear the Good News of Jesus.

- **Pray for your own courage and wisdom.**

    Your opportunity to re-present Jesus to them may come when you least expect it. Pray that you will be ready to respond to each opportunity with both the attitude and actions of Jesus.

Act

Starting _____ (when), I will begin praying every day for the following four people to come to know and follow Jesus:

_____   _____   _____

_____

Assess

- How difficult was it to pray for the four people on your list every day?
- Did you notice anything different about yourself, your relationship, or their willingness as a result of your prayers?

Next (suggested exercises)

Start Spiritual Conversations
Share the Good News
Make a Meal that Matters
A "Come as You Are" Invitation

Walk Don't Wave

*Be wise in the way you act toward outsiders; make the most of every opportunity.
Let your conversation be always full of grace, seasoned with salt, so that you may
know how to answer everyone.*
~ Colossians 4:5-6

The Gospels create a picture of Jesus drawing a crowd everywhere he went. It's easy to miss that people weren't just drawn to Jesus. Jesus was drawn to them. It was Jesus who called out to Peter, Andrew, James, and John as they were fishing (Matt. 4:18-22). When Jesus met a leper, he reached out to touch him (Luke 5:12-13). When Jesus saw a funeral procession, he was compelled by compassion to stop it and make the funeral unnecessary (Luke 7:11-15). It was Jesus who invited himself to Zacchaeus' house for dinner (Luke 19:1-5).

To be like Jesus is to be a person who is drawn to others, taking the initiative to begin conversations and relationships, knowing that every interaction is an opportunity to represent him. Some will find this more challenging than others. You may live in a place where you rarely see people, so you'll need to extend this exercise to your workplace or other places you frequently visit. You may be shy and need to stretch yourself to grow relationally in this way. You may not be the world's greatest conversationalist – the basic conversation starters below will help. The goal is simply to become a person who takes advantage of the opportunities daily life offers to engage with the people around you.

How

This simple practice begins with a commitment: When you see someone, don't just wave, instead walk to greet the person. These tips will help you get started:

- **"Hi, I'm Craig, what's your name?"**

  If you don't know the person already, start by introducing yourself and learning their name. Names go a long way to building relational bridges.

- **"How long have you _____?"**

  Be prepared to share a few facts about yourself and ask safe questions about them. Focus on facts first. How long they've lived or worked in a place, where they are from, and who they live with are good places to start.

- **"Hi _____! How's your day going?"**

  If you already know the person, simply take an interest in their life. Practice asking the question in a way that draws out a genuine response, not just the stereotypical "fine."

- **"What happened with _____?"**
  As you have multiple conversations with the same person, be sure to follow up with things they have already shared. If someone was sick, ask how the person is doing. If they were going on a trip, or doing something fun, ask how it was. If they had something big happening at work, ask how it turned out. Taking this kind of interest in others is where real friendship begins.

Act
For the next _____ (time), I will walk instead of wave whenever I see someone in my _____ (place). Keep track of how many times you can walk instead of wave in your daily routine.

Assess
- What did you find most difficult about walking instead of waving?
- What was the most interesting conversation you had?
- How would incorporating this habit into your daily life increase your opportunities to be like Jesus to the people around you?

Next (suggested exercises)
Make a Meal that Matters
Start a Group
Throw a Party
Have Fun with a Purpose

Have Fun with a Purpose

On the third day a wedding took place at Cana in Galilee. Jesus' mother was there, and Jesus and his disciples had also been invited to the wedding.
~ John 2:1-2

> Jesus and his disciples participated in "normal" life, fun, and celebrations. The attitudes and actions of Jesus are something we live out in our everyday lives. The more we can see our everyday lives as part of Jesus' mission, especially our fun, the more effective we will be in re-presenting Jesus to others.
>
> One of the challenges in our post-modern culture is that many people have been "evangelized" (they've had someone try to convince them about Jesus). As a result, many are skeptical about anyone who wants to tell them about their faith. Common interests can break down those barriers by helping you become a real person to whom they can relate.
>
> The challenge of the culture is made worse by our Christian culture. Christians run with church friends. Christians play golf...with church friends. Christians play softball...on the church team. The things you do for fun are some of your greatest opportunities to build relationships with people who don't know Jesus. Don't waste these opportunities by solely doing them with people who are already Christ-followers.

How
You won't need a lot of help here:

- **What do you enjoy doing?**

  It may be cycling, soccer, or Monday Night Football, outlet mall shopping, moms' meet-ups at the park, or listening to live music. If you like doing it, there is probably someone else who does too.

- **Go do it and include people who don't follow Jesus.**

  This is a great way to create relational momentum, when Christians in your group or Network are having fun along with those who don't know Jesus. Ask around, look around, or go to meetup.com. Find some people who are doing what you enjoy and join them. If you can't find a group–start one. Just make sure you invite everyone, not just your friends from church.

- **Establish the right social contract.**

  If you do something fun regularly with people far from God, don't go months without letting them know that faith is part of your life. If you cycle, for instance, with the same people for five months completely hiding your faith, it will seem strange or awkward to start "naturally" talking about spiritual matters, because that wasn't part of the social contract (or norm) established in the first couple of months.

Act
In the next _____ (time) I will begin _____ (activity) with _____ (who).

Assess
- What did you do?
- Whom did you meet?
- Will this be a good, ongoing way to increase relationship-building and spiritual impact?

Next (suggested exercises)
Pray 4:4
Make a Meal that Matters
Throw a Party

Make a Meal that Matters

Now the tax collectors and 'sinners' were all gathering around to hear him. But the Pharisees and the teachers of the law muttered, "This man welcomes sinners and eats with them."
~ Luke 15:1-2

Jesus didn't have a home, so he was always the guest, not the host. That didn't keep him from sharing meals with others. He was invited to Simon's house. He invited himself to Zacchaeus' house. These meals were more than food. They became the setting for important spiritual conversations.

The same will likely be true for you. One of the best ways to start a great conversation is to serve a meal. Sharing food opens the door for sharing life. If you have frantic visions of Martha Stewart, take a deep breath. You can make hot dogs into a meal that matters if you share them with friends.

The goal of this exercise isn't to serve a meal that impresses, but to start a conversation that matters. Whom you invite and what you talk about will matter more than what you serve.

How

Here are some really simple ideas for making a meal that matters:

- **Start with your calendar.**

    Find at least three dates that you could host a meal. Offering your guests more than one option will make it more likely that a meal actually happens.

- **Choose the right number.**

    If you're just getting acquainted, a meal for six, eight, or ten people may generate more conversation as different people make connections with each other. If you want to really get to know someone better, a meal for two to four is probably a better choice.

- **Choose the appropriate place.**

    An invitation to lunch at a restaurant may be a better first meal with a new acquaintance at work than an invitation to your home. But your neighbor might wonder why you wanted to go to the steakhouse when you've been bragging about your new grill for a month. Think about the people and then choose the best place.

- **Serve good food.**

    If you happen to be the next Iron Chef, go ahead and serve great food. For the rest of us, be content to serve good food. That's good enough. It's not a cooking competition, it's just a conversation starter.

- **Offer drinks with sensitivity.**

    Some of you reading this abstain from alcohol. Don't feel obligated to serve it. Be yourself and offer what is normal for you, especially if you are in your home. Some of you may drink alcohol in moderation. Be yourself and offer what is normal for you, yet with sensitivity to not make those who abstain feel uncomfortable, nor tempt those who may be tempted to drink too much or who may struggle in this area.

- **Make the conversation the centerpiece.**

    The quality of the conversation is what will make the meal matter (and even make the food taste better). Ask great questions and listen enthusiastically. Don't be afraid to start spiritual conversation. Most people are comfortable talking about spiritual things as long as they know it's safe. You may want to do the Start Spiritual Conversations exercise to get prepared.

- **Plan the next meal.**

    The best time to plan the next meal is before this one is over. If people have enjoyed good food and great conversation they will likely receive an invitation to do it again in the weeks or months ahead with favor.

Act

I/we will host a meal that matters in the next _____ (time).

I/We will invite:

Assess
- What was the hardest part of hosting a meal that matters?
- How did the meal go?
- What did you learn that would help you make this a more regular activity?

Next (suggested exercises)
Start a Group
Throw a Party
A "Come as You Are" Invitation

Throw a Party

While Jesus was having dinner at Matthew's house, many tax collectors and 'sinners' came and ate with him and his disciples.
~ Matthew 9:10

A party is universal human experience. In every culture and context people get together to enjoy each other around food, drink, music and dancing. If you grew up in church, you may have been taught parties that included the latter three were off limits. If you didn't grow up in church, you may have been to some parties that included all of the above in ways that weren't honoring to God. There is a way to bring these two experiences together for a purpose.

Jesus went to parties thrown by the religious (Luke 7:36) and non-religious (Matt. 9:10). In both cases, he knew why he was there–to show people the way to experience the fullness of life with God. As you build relationships with people who don't follow Jesus, you'll discover that a party can bring people who follow Jesus and people who don't together in a way that can lead to loving community.

How

There are all kinds of parties, even parties with a purpose. These ideas will assist you in making sure your party helps people build relationships and form community.

- **Start with a good party.**
  Inviting your friends who don't follow Jesus to come over and stand around staring at each other in silence, counting the minutes until they can politely leave, is counter productive. Make sure there is good food, lively music, and something to do that your guests will enjoy. If you're not a great party planner, team up with someone who is.

- **Invite a good mix of people.**
  One of the most important things that happens at a party with a purpose is relational connection. Get that off to a good start by thinking carefully whom you'll invite. Your neighbor plays softball, so invite the guys from your small group who play too. Your coworker has a new baby, so invite the couple from church who just had a baby too. You can't force the connections, but at least think like a matchmaker. Then when people come, introduce them to each other and point out commonalities!

- **Explain your purpose.**
  Be sure to let your friends who are Christ-followers know you're inviting a bunch of friends who aren't. Encourage them to make connections. As well, let your friends who don't follow Jesus know your "church friends" will be there. Give them reasons to want to meet each other that go beyond their differences in faith.

- **Know what's next.**

    If you're just getting started, it may be a big deal just to throw the party. If you're moving towards forming a Network, be prepared to tell people at the party what is next. It might be a Serve Party, or an invitation to a new small group, or just the next party or fun event. Whatever it is, build on the good experience to invite people to the next one.

Act

In the next _____ (time), I/we will throw a party and invite our friends who don't follow Jesus to meet our friends who do.

Assess
- How was the party?
- Who made connections?
- How could your next party be even better?

Next (suggested exercises)

Start a Group
Create a Rhythm
Have Fun with a Purpose
Throw a Serve Party

Start a Group

"Come," he replied, "and you will see." So they went and saw where he was staying, and spent that day with him. It was about the tenth hour.~ John 1:39

> Jesus often taught large crowds of people, but he began making disciples with a simple invitation, "Come and see." There are some people God has gifted to teach crowds like Jesus did, but not many. That doesn't mean you can't be part of making disciples. Every follower of Jesus can invite others to "come and see" and decide for themselves who they think he is.
>
> As you build relationships with people who aren't following Jesus, one of the most practical ways to invite them to "come and see" is to start a group. It is an opportunity for you to invite them to spend time intentionally exploring faith. If they are curious about spiritual things, this is an opportunity for them to ask questions and share thoughts in a safe environment.

How

Starting a group doesn't have to be complicated. Here are some tips for starting well:

- **Make an invitation list.**

    Start writing down names. List as many friends who are curious about Jesus as you can think of. Add a few names of friends who are following Jesus who would be willing to join in (maybe those reading and discussing *Unshockable Love* with you). A group will need at least five or six people to feel like a group, but try to list at least twice that many people to invite since some may not be able to come.

- **Start with an end in mind.**

    People are hesitant to make long-term or unending commitments. Suggest a six to eight week timeframe, and give them an easy "out." "I'm getting a group together for the next six weeks to explore questions about faith and spirituality—want to join us? You don't have to know anything in particular. It'll just be a safe place to wrestle with important questions we all have about life and God. It's just six weeks, so what do you have to lose?"

- **Choose a time and place.**

    Think about the people you want to invite and choose a time that would work for many of them. With today's schedules there won't be a perfect time, so be strategic. Choose a place that is comfortable for them. This may be your home, but it might be a coffee shop or restaurant, clubhouse or bar.

- **Choose a focus for a time.**

    People will most likely respond better to an invitation to read a book together or talk about a specific topic than to just "come to a group." There are lots of great resources for starting small groups for exploring faith. We've written *Investigating the Way of Christ* and *Velocity* for these kinds of groups.

    (You can download both free at www.gatewayleaders.com/resources.)

- **Pray for favor.**

    Before Nehemiah asked for the king's help, he prayed for favor (Neh. 1:11). Before you invite your friends to your group, follow his example. Spend some time praying through your list and asking God to give you favor with each person as you invite them.

- **Invite them to come.**

    In the age of social media, this could seem a little old fashioned, but there is nothing like a personal invitation. That's not to say posting your group on Facebook or sending the info out on Twitter is bad, but take the time and make the effort to invite each person on your list face to face or by phone. Follow up the positive responses with reminders–here you can use whatever form of communication is familiar to your group.

- **Create a safe place.**

    The best yet the most challenging thing you'll experience is having lots of your friends who don't follow Jesus come to your group. Let them know you're glad they came by welcoming them and their ideas. This can be hard because sometimes they will say things that you know are the opposite of what the Bible teaches. Don't feel like you need to tell them they are wrong. Just keep pointing the group towards Jesus and to what the Bible does say. Jesus is able to draw them to himself.

Act

On _____ (date), I/we will start a group to focus on _____ (topic) for _____ (length of time). I/we will invite the following people to come:

For small groups or Network core groups: We will start a group where our friends can explore faith on _____ (topic) for _____ (length of time). We will invite the following people to come:

Assess
- How did people respond to your invitation?
- How did the people who came respond to the group?
- What is the best next step for your new group?

Next (suggested exercises)
Throw a Party
Create a Rhythm

Check Your Connections

When he had gone indoors, the blind men came to him, and he asked them, "Do you believe that I am able to do this?" "Yes, Lord," they replied. Then he touched their eyes and said, "According to your faith will it be done to you;" and their sight was restored. Jesus warned them sternly, "See that no one knows about this." But they went out and spread the news about him all over that region.
~ Matthew 9:28-31

At this point in Jesus' ministry he told the blind men to not proclaim what he had done because his time had not yet come. They were so excited they couldn't keep themselves from telling everyone they knew. He later commanded all of us to tell everyone about him. What if we were as bold as the blind men? We should be, because Jesus has not only given us eyes to see, but life eternal.

What would it look like if you spread the Good News of Jesus to everyone you know? Consider another question: do you know who you know? Maybe put another way, do you know how many people you know? Would you be telling 5, 50, or 500 about Jesus if you were one of the blind men? When they take the time to check their relational connections, most people are surprised by how many people they know. More amazing is the relational potential of a small group or Network when added up together.

How

This is a very simple and practical activity–make a list of people you know as well as their relational and spiritual potential.

1. **Make a list.**

    Here are a few a places to look:

    - If you have an address book, start there.
    - If you have a cell phone dump your contact list.
    - Export your email contact list.
    - Download your Facebook data to get a list of your friends.
    - Download your twitter followers.

2. **Consider your relational potential.**

    About now, you may be surprised how long the list is. You can make it more manageable by asking a simple question. "Would you invite this person to an event?" (for example, a BBQ in a park). You're looking for the people where there is enough relational potential to invite them to do something with you.

3. **Discern their spiritual potential.**

   Looking at the list of people with whom you have relational potential, ask yourself, "Where are they spiritually?" You should be able to put most of them into one of these five categories:

   - Antagonistic: They have an unfavorable view of God and the Church and react negatively to any conversation about spiritual things (and may also be committed to another faith).
   - Apathetic: They aren't against Jesus, they just don't have any interest in getting to know him or anything spiritual in nature.
   - Curious: They are curious about Jesus and willing to be part of spiritual conversations or activities.
   - Committed: They are committed followers of Jesus who are deepening their faith as they use their gifts to lead and serve others.
   - Don't know: In spite of the relationship you have with them, you have no idea about their spiritual beliefs or practices.

4. **What's next?**

You can take this exercise one step further and turn it into an action plan by asking one more question: What's next? Based on the quality of your relationship and where they are spiritually, what would be a next step in your relationship with them? If they are antagonistic or apathetic, it may be just to invite them to share a meal or join you in an activity. If they are ready to discover faith, maybe an invitation to your small group or Network event is what's next. If a committed Christian, maybe it's casting vision to about being on mission with you and a Network of people.

Act

In the next _____ (time), I will make a relational or spiritual connection with at least _____ (#) people on my list who are not following Jesus.

Assess

- How did you react to the number of people you could list?
- What opportunities for building relationships or creating community can you discover by looking at your list?

Next (suggested exercises)

Pray 4:4
Make a Meal that Matters
Throw a Party
Have Fun with a Purpose

Make Room

*Be very careful, then, how you live--not as unwise but as wise, making the
most of every opportunity, because the days are evil.*
~ Ephesians 5:15-16

It seem like Jesus was always with people. Crowds followed him, sometimes even when he was trying to get away. Depending on how you feel about crowds and people, it may sound exhilarating or just plain exhausting. It's doubtful you'll end up with crowds following you to work or the grocery store, but if you are going to invest time and energy in building relationships, you will need to make room.

Relationships take time. The American way is just to add and add and add people and things to your schedule until there just isn't room for anything else. The problem is, you've probably already done that, which means there are some things you'll likely need to stop doing.

Going on mission with Jesus isn't just an activity or program you add to your schedule. Becoming like Jesus in attitude and action will mean learning to make the most of every opportunity, including things you're already doing like work and school, to build relationships with people far from God.

The goal of this exercise is to help you make room for being on mission in your relationships. The challenge isn't making the plan, it's actually re-arranging your life around investing in and serving others.

How

Here are three simple steps you can take to evaluate your schedule and take action to make room for relationships.

1. **Keep doing**

    Make a list of the activities that are currently part of your daily, weekly, or monthly routine (work, school, sports, clubs…) which are great environments for building relationships with people far from God.

2. **Start doing**

    If your current activities are not creating enough opportunities to build relationships, make a list of at least two to three things you could start doing to intentionally invest in people and relationships.

3. **Stop doing**

   Whether you're going to be more intentional about activities you're already doing, or start doing some new ones, you will most likely need to make more room for the people you are building relationships with. Make a list of things you will stop doing to make room in your life for more relationships. Try to eliminate 5 to 10 hours a week of existing activities. This may be as simple as turning off the TV, or as complex as shrinking your work life back to something less than 60 hours a week!

Act

I will implement my plan for making room for the next _____ (time) and then re-evaluate the relational space in my life.

Assess

- Which was more difficult—starting a new activity or stopping an old one?
- Where did you find the most relational opportunity—in something you were already doing or something new you started doing?

Next (suggested exercises)

Start a Group
Create a Rhythm
Have Fun with a Purpose

Create a Rhythm

He went to Nazareth, where he had been brought up, and on the Sabbath day he went into the synagogue, as was his custom. And he stood up to read.
~ Luke 4:16

> It may seem strange, but even Jesus had habits. It didn't seem to matter what town he was in, or whose party he was at on Friday night. If it was Saturday he went to the synagogue. Habits are a powerful force in our lives. Yes, bad habits can be very destructive, but on the other hand, good habits simplify our lives. Have you ever thought about how much work it would be to shower, brush your teeth, and get dressed if you didn't have a habit or pattern? Habits are like rhythm, when you've got it you can move from one thing to the next without having to think about it.
>
> As you begin to go on mission with Jesus, you will need to develop some new habits or rhythms for your life. These new rhythms will keep you connected to God and focused on others. The hard part isn't keeping them, it's creating them.
>
> The goal of this exercise is to help you intentionally shape a new rhythm of life around being on mission with Jesus to re-present him and help restore the world around you.

How

Use this simple process to form a new rhythm that creates missional momentum. If you are working through the Action Guide with partners, do this activity together to create a rhythm for your group or Network as well as yourself.

1. **Start by prioritizing what's important.**

    Things like...

    - Passionate prayer.
    - Meeting new people.
    - Creating space for community to form.
    - Serving your neighbors.
    - Spiritual conversations.
    - Eating meals together.

2. **Order them into daily, weekly and monthly rhythms.**

    For example...

    - Order each day around prayer and intentional time for spiritual conversations.
    - Order each week around community, serving, and eating with others.
    - Order each month around opportunities to meet new people.

3. **Practice your new rhythm until it feels natural.**
   - If there is something in your planned rhythm that keeps tripping you up, assess why. You may need to give that activity extra focus until you get it, or you may need to adjust the plan because it turns out to be unrealistic.
   - Don't expect to feel comfortable the first day, week, or even month. Re-ordering your life and creating a new rhythm that sustains mission will take time.
   - Give yourself grace. Each day is an opportunity to start again – seize it!

Act
I/we will keep the following rhythm on mission with Jesus:

After _____ (time), I/we will evaluate to see how it is working.

Assess
- How do you feel about forming a new rhythm of life?
- How could this rhythm help you, and your group, be more effective on living out the attitude and actions of Jesus?

Next (suggested exercises)
Start a Group
Find a Cause to Serve
Have Fun with a Purpose

Serve Someone

So he got up from the meal, took off his outer clothing, and wrapped a towel around his waist. After that, he poured water into a basin and began to wash his disciples' feet, drying them with the towel that was wrapped around him.
~ John 13:4-5

Jesus served countless people. He fed the crowds so they wouldn't have to find food. He was constantly healing the sick that were brought to him. There is something unique about this picture in John 13. Jesus was with his closest friends. They were having dinner and no one had washed their feet–a Jewish tradition before a meal. Either no one had noticed, or if they had, they ignored the need because it felt "beneath" them. But not Jesus. He got up from the meal that had already started and washed his friends' feet. And then he said, "I have given you an example to follow" (John 13:15).

Almost everyone likes to be served. Serving others? It's time consuming, often inconvenient, and sometimes humiliating. Yes, it was all of those things for Jesus and more. If we want to be like him, we must follow his example like he told us to do. The question is not, "Can you serve others?" for everyone can serve someone. The question is, "Are you willing?"

How

At one level this is easy, just serve someone. At another level, it can be a big challenge to re-orient your day to what someone else needs instead of what you are already doing. Here are some ideas for stretching your serve muscles:

- **Decide in advance to serve whatever need you see.**

  This exercise is as much about your attitude as your actions. You might see that a co-worker needs help carrying something–it's not hard to be an extra pair of hands. The key is whether you have the eyes to see and the willingness to be available. So start your day with a decision, "Today I will look for needs, big or small, and serve them when I see them."

- **Pray for open eyes and a willing heart.**

  There is a reason you don't see needs and serve them. You are, like all of humanity, selfish. Becoming a servant is the work of the Holy Spirit in you, so ask him to give you both eyes to see the needs, and a willing heart to serve them when you do.

- **Don't hesitate, just serve.**

  You are most likely to do something when you first feel the impulse. If you pay attention, you may discover that you are talking yourself out of serving–because you're too busy, too tired, or too important to do what needs to be done. Stop listening to those voices. When you see a need, don't hesitate, just serve.

Act
For the next _____ (time), I will look for and commit to serving needs wherever and whenever I see them. (Write down the people and ways you were able to serve when you opened your eyes and heart to see and respond).

Assess
- Were you surprised by how many needs you saw?
- What resistance did you feel toward serving?
- What effect did serving spontaneously have on your heart?

Next (suggested exercises)
Go to the Hurting
Find a Cause to Serve
Throw a Serve Party

Throw a Serve Party

As evening approached, the disciples came to him and said, "This is a remote place, and it's already getting late. Send the crowds away, so they can go to the villages and buy themselves some food." Jesus replied, "They do not need to go away. You give them something to eat."
~ Matthew 14:15-16

This exercise is based on the "Try This" activity in Chapter 12 on p. 235 in *Unshockable Love*.

> Jesus' disciples saw a need. There were a lot of people, and they were all hungry. They also saw a solution–send them away to go find food. Jesus could see the people were hungry too, but he saw another need–his disciples needed to have enough faith to serve. We don't just experience the kingdom of God when our needs are met, we also experience the kingdom of God when we meet the needs of others. Both are an exercise of our faith.
>
> For this reason, serving is a great way for people who are not following Jesus to experience his kingdom. Don't miss the opportunity for them to discover faith through serving with you. As you serve side by side, they will have an opportunity to see your heart as well as experience what it means to be like Jesus.

Act

This exercise will get your group and your friends who aren't yet following Jesus serving together. Here is how:

- **Identify a need.**
  Look for something in your neighborhood that you and a group of friends could do in a day. You won't be putting an end to homelessness, but you might clean up the yard for an elderly or disabled person. You might help someone move. You might paint a room or two at a local homeless shelter.

- **Set a date.**
  You'll want to include as many people as possible. However, waiting until everyone can make it most likely means you'll never do it.

- **Invite your friends.**
  Remember the goal here is not just to get your group to serve. Your goal is to get the Christians in your group to invite friends who don't follow Jesus to serve with you.

- **Have the supplies ready.**
  There is probably at least one person in your group who is organized (just peek in their fridge or kitchen pantry). Put them in charge of supplies. Inviting people to serve, and then showing up without the needed supplies, is like throwing a party and guests arrive only to find out there's no food. Be prepared. If necessary, pass a bowl to collect enough money to buy the supplies.

- **Have fun.**

  That's right, when the day comes to serve, have fun! Unless there is some compelling reason why laughter is out of place, put someone in charge of making sure there is plenty of it. Serving isn't drudgery–it's joyful!

- **Debrief.**

  After you've finished serving for the day, get everyone together for some good food and spend time debriefing, discussing these questions:

  - How did serving others make you feel?
  - What kind of responses did others have to our serving?
  - In what ways has this experience inspired or challenged you?
  - Depending on the level of relationship, this might be a great time to inject a spiritual question like, "How does serving others reflect the heart of God?," or, "Why do you think Jesus said, 'the greatest will become a servant?'"

Act

On _____ (date), I/we will invite _____ (names) to serve with me/us by doing:

_____

Assess

- How successful was your activity in terms of the outcome for those you served? How successful in terms of the outcome for your group?

- What did you learn that will help you lead serving opportunities more effectively in the future?

- What kind of conversations did you have with the people you invited to serve with you?

Next (suggested exercises)

Start a Group
Create a Rhythm
Find a Cause to Serve

Find a Cause to Serve

The Spirit of the Lord is on me, because he has anointed me to preach good news to the poor. He has sent me to proclaim freedom for the prisoners and recovery of sight for the blind, to release the oppressed, to proclaim the year of the Lord's favor.
~ Luke 4:18-19

> Jesus came to bring good news, especially for those whose lives were covered in the mud of poverty, imprisonment, blindness and oppression. The world hasn't changed much. In fact, there are even more people today in need of Jesus' good news. Billions of them live in poverty, suffer from oppression or addiction, and are physically ill or have disabilities.
>
> As a follower of Jesus, this can be overwhelming, especially in a connected world where every human tragedy, regardless of where it happens, finds its way onto our screens. It's tempting to throw your hands in the air and say, "What difference could I possibly make?" For 7 billion people the answer may be "not much," but for a few people with specific needs in your own neighborhood or city, you could be the one who brings good news and God's restorative kingdom ways.
>
> Do you (and your group or Network core) have a cause to serve? Inviting neighbors or coworkers still exploring faith to come serve others with you can be a powerful catalyst for everyone's spiritual growth.

How

You and your Network can make a big difference by joining a cause or finding a cause to serve in your community. Here are some tips to figure out how:

- **Start by seeing needs.**

    If you haven't already, do the "Seeing Needs" exercise on page 15 in this Action Guide.

- **Find out who is serving already.**

    It's easy to be overwhelmed by needs, but you might be equally surprised to find out how many people and groups are already serving in your community. You can go online, call the local Chamber of Commerce or City Hall, ask around at schools or other churches. Even a little detective work will likely produce a long list of people already serving.

- **Connect with your passion.**

    Consider doing the "Heart Storming" exercise on page 49. Ask, "Where do my/our passions connect with needs in our community?" You'll naturally find it easier to connect and sustain involvement with people you share a passion with.

- **Ask how you can help.**

  There is no better way to announce, "Here come the Pharisees" than for a group of Christians to show up with a "We're here to save the day" attitude. Humbly offer your help with no strings attached.

- **Invite people exploring faith to serve with you.**

  Once you or your group has served a few times to know how best to meet needs, invite those far from God you're building relationships with. Serving together can be fertile ground for spiritual conversations.

- **Keep trying.**

  Don't be discouraged if your first attempt to serve isn't well received. It won't really make sense, but it happens. Keep praying and keep asking God to lead you to a cause that really connects and makes a difference.

Act

In the next _____ (time), I/we will identify a cause in our community and offer to help in whatever way I/we can.

In the next _____ (time), I/we will invite the following people (who may still be far from God) to come serve with me/us (names):

Assess

- Were you surprised by what people were already doing in your community?
- How was your offer to help received?
- What kinds of conversations came up while serving?

Next (suggested exercises)

Seeing Needs
Invite Others
Throw a Serve Party

Go to the Hurting

*Therefore, as God's chosen people, holy and dearly loved, clothe yourselves
with compassion, kindness, humility, gentleness and patience.*
~ Colossians 3:12

This exercise is based on the "Try This" activity in Chapter 7 on p. 145 in *Unshockable Love*.

> How do you react when people are hurting? Are you a person who naturally moves toward them wanting to help in any way you can? Are you a person who backs away, unsure what to do or say? Are you a person who just looks the other way, hoping not to get involved in someone else's mess?
>
> Jesus never turned away from a hurting person, and he met lots of them. Time and time again he moved toward someone who was hurting. To be like Jesus is to be a person who also moves toward the hurting. This raises a common fear. "What if they need more help than I can give? I can't heal everyone like Jesus did!" This is true. Compassion begins with what you hold in your heart. First, care about them enough to move toward their pain, and then help as you are able without becoming responsible for their healing.
>
> This exercise will challenge you to go to those who are hurting, not to fix them or solve their problem, but simply to let them know you care.

How

You shouldn't have to look too far to find someone who is hurting–especially if you have been doing these exercises. There are hurting people all around you. These tips will help you move toward the hurting:

- **Pray for eyes to see.**

  Commit to start your day asking for eyes to see the hurting people around you. Some pain is obvious, but many people hide their hurts. If you are willing, the Holy Spirit will show you when and where people you see every day are hurting.

- **Pray for a heart to respond.**

  The more you see, the more you may wish you didn't. Ask God to give you his compassion for others in a way that draws you to them rather than repels you away from them.

- **Be present.**

  Start with a simple expression of understanding, "I can see you are hurting." Offer to listen, but don't pry. Be careful not to say too much and unintentionally amplify their pain.

- **Be willing to give what you have.**
  If someone is hurting because they are hungry, it is probably within your means to feed them. If someone is hurting because they've lost a loved one, it's obviously beyond your means to bring their loved one back. What you always have to give is your presence, but you can't always solve their problem. Know the difference and be willing to give what you have and be okay with not offering what is beyond your ability to provide.

Act
For the next _____ (time), I will pray for the opportunity to move toward someone who is hurting, and respond when God shows me an opportunity. I will try to simply be present and care, rather than try to fix or solve their problem.

Assess
- What did you find most difficult about this exercise?
- What happened as a result of moving toward someone who was hurting?
- How has this experience helped you see others with the eyes of Jesus?

Next (suggested exercises)
Prayer Walk
Seeing Needs
Serve Someone
Find a Cause to Serve

Heart Storming

*O Jerusalem, Jerusalem, you who kill the prophets and stone those sent to you,
how often I have longed to gather your children together, as a hen gathers her chicks
under her wings, but you were not willing!*
~ Luke 13:34

> Take a few minutes to read Luke 13:31-34. Jesus was being warned, "Run away, your life is in danger!" He responded by saying he can't do that. He must keep going. Why? Why didn't he take the warning and get out of danger? Jesus was a passionate person. His heart was broken for his people and especially the city of Jerusalem. He wanted to rescue them, but the people weren't willing.
>
> What about you? What breaks your heart? What are you passionate about? What would you keep doing even if someone threatened your life if you didn't stop?
>
> This exercise, taken from p. 235 of *Unshockable Love* and part of the *Soul Storming Guidebook*,* will help you answer those questions.

How

This activity is written for a group (for example, the group you are reading and discussing *Unshockable Love* with). You could adapt it to use on your own, although we'd highly recommend discussing it with at least one other person.

- **Heart storming**

  Have each person write out an answer to the question, "What really breaks your heart about what you see around you?"

  Think about your neighborhood. What's broken there? Think about the places you frequent or pass by, or places you know in your city or area—what would God want restored? Think about the people around you. What's most broken in their lives? What would it mean to see God's kingdom come to restore what's broken?

- **Life storming**

  Next, give each person time to answer this question: "What gives you life?"

  What do you love to do? If you had no fear, and all the resources you needed, what would you do? What things have happened to you in life that give you a passion for helping others in the same situation? Maybe it's overcoming an addiction and you're passionate about helping others break free. Maybe you suffered abuse and would love to help others heal from the same. Maybe you felt worthless as a kid and passionately want to give value to kids who feel abandoned or unwanted.

- **Prioritize**

    Finally, have everyone take their lists home and rank the top five things that break their hearts and their top five life passions. Then at the next gathering, give each person ten minutes to share these top fives. Take time afterward to discuss what God's Spirit might be showing you as a group or Network. Where might you serve together? What should you try? How could your different gifts and experiences support one another as you serve your world?

*If you'd like to experience the full process, the *Soul Storming Guidebook*, by Jason Heriford, is available on Amazon.

Act
I/we will do the Heart Storming exercise starting on _____ (date).

Assess
- Did anything end up on your top five list that surprised you?
- How different would your life look if you pursued your passions?
- How would you be more like Jesus if you pursued your passions?

Next (suggested exercises)
Find a Cause to Serve
Throw a Serve Party
Have Fun with a Purpose

Start Spiritual Conversations

When a Samaritan woman came to draw water, Jesus said to her, "Will you give me a drink?"
~ John 4:7

This exercise is based on the "Try This" activity in Chapter 6 on p. 123 in *Unshockable Love*.

> It seems like such a simple request, "Will you give me a drink?" Jesus was able to turn that simple question into a powerful, life-changing spiritual conversation. If you read the Gospels, you'll notice that Jesus asked lots of questions, hundreds of them in fact. Our spiritual conversations might improve if we became like him by learning to ask more questions. Many people are afraid to talk about Jesus because they don't know what to say. You can have great spiritual conversations without "saying" anything–just ask questions.
>
> The goal of this exercise is to learn to use simple questions to start spiritual conversations. Developing this skill will give you the opportunity to have many more spiritual conversations with those who are not following Jesus.

How

You most likely have casual conversations with people every day. Often these conversations follow familiar and safe social patterns, like the weather, current events, or sports. Use these ideas to move some of these conversations toward spiritual topics.

- **Ask simple questions.**

    "Where did you grow up?" "What was your family like growing up?" "What's your spiritual background?" "Was your family religious growing up? What was that like for you?" "What are you passionate about?" "Have you ever thought about God—what thoughts do you have?" "If you could do anything, what would you do?" "Do you consider yourself a spiritual person? Do you know anyone who is really spiritual?" These questions invite people to talk about their own experiences and their deeper desires in a non-threatening way. There is no right or wrong answer–you're just asking about what they've experienced.

- **Listen actively.**

    It seems obvious, but pay attention. Look at them while they talk. If there is a moment of silence, wait patiently. If they say something you don't understand, ask about it. Everyone values a friend who cares enough to listen. Be curious and interested. Ask follow up questions. Make it your point to encourage them to talk at as deep a level as they are willing to go. Most people have never had anyone interested enough in them to draw them out in this way—it's powerful!

- **Ask more questions.**

  Resist the temptation to tell your story unless you are specifically asked–even then keep it brief. Think about what you've heard and ask more questions that will take their story even further.

- **Value the person and the conversation.**

  At the end of the conversation be sure to thank them for telling you about themselves. Tell them you value them sharing their story. Communicating value will open the door to more conversations in the future.

Act
In the next _____ (time), I will use spiritual questions to try to start at least _____ (#) spiritual conversations. (Write down the names and details of each conversation, and what you learned about each person's story. This will give you a more informed way to pray for them as well. God will use that to open deeper conversations.)

Assess
- What did you find most difficult about this exercise?
- How did others respond to your spiritual questions?
- How has this exercise prepared you for future spiritual conversations?

Next (suggested exercises)
Share the Good News
Make a Meal that Matters
Start a Group

Listen for Their Spiritual Story

*When Jesus saw him lying there and learned that he had been in this condition
for a long time, he asked him, "Do you want to get well?"*
~ John 5:6

> Jesus was asked 183 questions, directly answered only 3, but asked 307 questions. He listened and learned about the needs of people in order to discern where the Father was working (John 5:6,19). If you're going to treat people like Jesus did, you must not only cross divides to dignify people by asking questions and dialoguing, you must listen deeply to try to understand their needs, their points of pain, and their concerns. This will greatly help you see where God might be at work, drawing them to himself, and even where your story or your Christian friend's story intersects their story. Pharisees just talk *at* people. Jesus didn't do that. He asked thought-provoking questions, listened, and cared about the needs and points of pain of those he encountered. This was often where Jesus started with people—at their greatest need or point of pain. This exercise will help you learn to ask questions and listen for the spiritual stories of people you're building relational momentum with. Everyone has a spiritual story, even an atheist. There are things that happened in their past that shaped who they are, how they think about God, themselves, people, the meaning of life—some were good and from God, some were evil and set up destructive thought patterns. Understanding how people got to where they are today can help you guide them toward the truth about God and his good intentions for them.

How

This exercise will most likely be done over a series of conversations you have with the person, asking questions and picking up on clues. Think of it like spiritual detective work—taking interest in who this person is and the clues to how and why they formed the spiritual perspectives they have today. You may have to find creative ways to engage in conversation to answer these questions, but try to discover the answer to as many of these spiritual profile questions as you can:

- Where did they grow up and what was their family like?
- What was their relationship with their mom and dad like growing up?
- Who had the most positive impact on them growing up? The most negative?
- What was their spiritual background growing up?
- If they had a churched background, was that positive or negative—how?
- What most shaped their spiritual beliefs today?
- How do they view God and what led them to that view?
- What most shaped their view of life and what it's about?
- What has wounded them in life? (This is often a key to spiritual beliefs and barriers or places God wants to heal.)

Act
I will seek to answer at least half these questions in writing for _____ (name) or _____ (second name) by _____ (date).

Assess
- How would you summarize this person's spiritual story?
- How did doing this spiritual detective work affect your attitude toward that person?
- Where do you think God might be working in this person, or how might you engage in a spiritual conversation based on what you learned?

Next (suggested exercises)
Telling Your Spiritual Story
Share the Good News

Telling Your Spiritual Story

Then Paul said, "I am a Jew, born in Tarsus, a city in Cilicia, and I was brought up and educated here in Jerusalem under Gamaliel. As his student, I was carefully trained in our Jewish laws and customs. I became very zealous to honor God in everything I did, just like all of you today. And I persecuted the followers of the Way, hounding some to death, arresting both men and women..."
~ Acts 22:2-4

> In the book of Acts, we see multiple instances of Christians telling their personal spiritual stories as a way to share their faith with those not following Jesus (Acts 22, 26). Because your story is your own, telling it is often the most non-threatening, non-preachy way to talk about the message of faith in Christ. Your story can also connect with someone else's story. As you are building relational momentum, learning to listen to another person's story, and asking spiritual questions, you will have opportunity as the Spirit leads to naturally tell your story. You need to be prepared to give reason for the hope you personally have (2 Tim. 4:2). If you take the time to write it down, this will help you be able to convey your story without rambling on forever. Usually a person will start to check out after about three minutes unless you make it interactive. That's why we want to help you be prepared to tell your story well. If you are prepared, then you can improvise, stop and dialogue, yet still have an outline in your head to guide you. The process below will help you shape your story. Know it well, but don't try to memorize it word for word—you don't want to come off scripted or rehearsed. Ironically, being prepared helps you to be more natural and conversational.

How

These steps will help you prepare your story.

Take time to write down answers to these questions:

1. **What was your life like before Christ?**

    You can't talk about your whole life in three to five minutes, so pick a few themes that would relate to most people without faith. Maybe you were all about success and accomplishment, or beauty and getting attention, or sports, or money, or being the life of the party—proving yourself as the wild child. Maybe you grew up in church, but it was more ritual than relationship. Write down what motivated and drove your life before letting God be God. Before you started following Christ, what were you banking on to one day have the security, worth, love, or happiness we all long for?

2. **What led you to make Christ your forgiver and leader?**

    How did the things you were living for begin to let you down? How did they show signs of being a weak foundation on which to build your life? God usually gets our attention when "playing God" starts to not work so well—did that happen with you? This will be your best touch-point with others—connecting to the need we all have for relationship with God.

When did you first hear the message of Christ? This is your opportunity to convey the three themes of the Good News (in Chapter 8) without sounding preachy—how did you hear it? Weave it into your story.

What were your initial reactions? Fears? Concerns? Misunderstandings about God's intentions? What struggles did you have to work through before opening your heart to Christ? What helped your attitude change, and what opened your heart up to God's offer of relationship?

What did you do to enter into relationship with God? This is a chance to clarify that it's by faith, and God has removed every barrier between us and him except our pride. A simple, humble prayer acknowledging our need for forgiveness and his guidance is all he requires—include how you did this.

3. **How has your life been since beginning a relationship with God?**

   What's your life been like in relationship with God? Be specific about changes you've experienced. Reflect on the fruits of his Spirit you've seen grow in your life (see Galatians 5:22), but also trials and challenges you've faced. Think about the spiritual aspects of life—relational growth, internal growth, facing fears and failures, trials or troubles.

- Avoid "Christianese."
  Read through your story looking for Christianese—terms that won't connect with or be understood by someone exploring faith. Use Appendix A in *Unshockable Love* to find ways to explain Christian terms in normal language.

- Edit and practice.
  Now edit down what you've written to about three or four minutes when read aloud. Instead of memorizing every word, highlight key words or key ideas. Now try to say it out loud glancing at your notes. Then try to say it with no notes. Once you've done this, find a Christian to share it with to help you feel natural and comfortable telling it.

Act

I will write out my spiritual story by _____ (date).

I have practiced telling it in three to five minutes with another Christian giving me feedback: _____ (date you shared it). (Practicing with a group member or spiritual running partner is best, but otherwise just find someone safe who will give you feedback.)

I have shared my spiritual story with someone not following Christ _____ (date you actually shared your story).

Assess

- What was most difficult about this exercise for you?
- What was most encouraging to you?
- How did people respond when you shared your spiritual story?

Next (suggested exercises)

Share the Good News

Share the Good News

He said to them, "Go into all the world and preach the good news to all creation."
~ Mark 16:15

This exercise is based on the "Try This" activity in Chapter 8 on p. 169 in *Unshockable Love*.

> Jesus came to bring Good News, and he sends us to do the same (Matt 4:23, John 20:21). Too often people who are not following Jesus feel like the message they get from Christians is bad news. This may feel discouraging to you, but it creates a great opportunity. You can bring good news to someone who isn't expecting it!
>
> The goal of this exercise is to help you tell the Good News to people you have relationships with. Don't worry about convincing them about what is true or right. This is not your job. Jesus explains very clearly that convincing is the working of the Holy Spirit (John 16:8-11). Your privilege is getting to be a part of delivering the Good News.

How

Sharing the Good News doesn't need to be complicated. In fact, it should be one of the most natural things you do as a follower of Jesus. Here is how you can do it:

- **Prepare to tell God's story.**

    Take the time to read the summaries of the three themes of the Gospel in Chapter 8 of *Unshockable Love* (p. 147). Highlight or underline words or phrases that you want to communicate. Try to write the essential ideas on a single sticky note. This will help you keep your summary of the Good News simple and straightforward. Practice conveying these three themes until you can say them from memory in your own words. The goal is to get comfortable enough with where you're going that you can stop and dialogue, then pick back up where you left off—that makes sharing God's Good News more conversational and less preachy. Preparation will help you come across more relaxed! (The text box summaries in Chapter 8 will give examples of how I've often conveyed each theme.)

- **Pray for the opportunity.**

    Now that you're ready, pray for the opportunity to share. If you have been praying for specific people already (like in the Pray 4:4 exercise on page 23), you may want to pray for the opportunity to share the Good News with one of these people in the very near future. Sharing the Good News is most natural when you're just casually hanging out together.

- **Share with enthusiasm.**
    Remember that people sense what is in your heart. It will seem confusing to hear Good News from someone who seems to be bored or scared. The most natural way to share Good News is enthusiastically. Before you go, reread Chapter 8 to remember how God feels about all people.

Act
For the next _____ (time), I will pray for the opportunity to share the Good News with someone who is not following Jesus, and I will respond to the opportunity when it comes.

Assess
- What did you find most difficult about this exercise?
- What was the result of sharing the Good News?
- How has this exercise prepared you to share the Good News more often?

Next (suggested exercises)
Check Your Connections
Pray 4:4
Make a Meal that Matters
Start a Group

A "Come as You Are" Invitation

When Jesus had finished saying these things, the crowds were amazed at his teaching.
~ Matthew 7:28

This exercise is based on the "Try This" activity in Chapter 13 on p. 254 in *Unshockable Love*.

> Jesus taught in the temple (Luke 21:37) and in the local synagogue (Luke 13:10). Jesus also taught on the hillsides (Matt. 5:1) and beside the lake (Mark 4:1). These are where the crowds came, because Jesus taught both with authority and in a way that everyone could understand. Jesus taught people about God the Father in relationship to real life (Matt. 5-7).
>
> There is something unique about hearing a message in a crowd. You are able to think about the words of the speaker differently than the same words spoken by a close friend over coffee. Both venues are effective and needed in order to communicate the Good News in ways people not following Jesus can understand. Too often the listening crowd includes only those people who are already convinced. Even worse, the message is only accessible to them. In order to help people follow Jesus, we need to invite them to "come as they are" to places where they can learn about the Way of Christ.

How

If you've made it this far in the Action Guide, two things are most likely true. First you have been building relational momentum with friends who are not followers of Jesus, and second, you are probably part of a church or faith community. Now is the time to bring those two things together. Here are a few practical steps you can take to do that:

- **Identify who is curious or at least open.**

    As you build relationships, you'll begin to notice that some people are more open or even outright curious than others. This is normal and may be the Holy Spirit working in their hearts to draw them toward Jesus. Be sensitive to this and aware of who is ready to explore faith.

- **Pick a date.**

    Hopefully your church has a calendar or schedule of what's coming up. Look for a Sunday with a message or topic that would be easy to invite someone to for the first time. If your church presents messages in a series, then the start of a new series is often a good time. (The Sunday of the annual business meeting is probably not!)

- **Invite your friends to join you.**

    With a date in mind, start inviting the friends you believe are curious or open. Be sure to invite them to come with you or meet you there–many people are uncomfortable going to a new place alone. An expert guide makes the experience better.

If you're not sure your church is a good place to explore faith, ask for their help: "Would you help me and my friends with a project? We're trying to figure out what would need to change in our church service to help people feel comfortable exploring faith if they wanted to. Would you come and just give us feedback about what would help you if you were interested in exploring Christian faith?"

*The Alpha Course could be another option for your church or Network to host as a "come as you are" venue for exploring faith. Check out www.alphausa.org.

- **Don't give up.**

    Don't be discouraged if they say "no" to your first invitation. People are busy and church is uncomfortable for many, and so they will have many reasons and excuses for not being able to come. Don't take it personally. Jesus said, "It's not you they are rejecting, but me" (Luke 10:16). Be prepared to invite them multiple times. It usually takes five to seven invites before someone finally comes.

- **Invite them to hang out afterwards.**

    Spending time afterwards gives them an opportunity to debrief, and it gives you an opportunity to learn from them. This is important—this is not your chance to make sure they got it. It is your chance to ask questions. How did you feel? What was confusing? What was most interesting or helpful?

- **Invite them to come again.**

    There are people who come the first time and say "yes" to Jesus. There are others who come for months, even years, before they say "yes." Be sensitive to their pace and continue to invite them even if they come infrequently.

Act
I will invite _____ (names) to join me on _____ (date).

Assess
- How did your friends respond to your invitation? What did you learn about making effective invites?
- What did you learn from those who came with you? How do their experiences challenge you to see church differently?

Next (suggested exercises)
Make a Meal that Matters
Start a Group
Share the Good News

Have Powerful Conversations

Above all else, guard your heart, for it is the wellspring of life.
~ Proverbs 4:23

All people have hopes and dreams—God made us that way. He put a sense of eternity in our hearts (Ecc. 3:11). We all long for purpose and meaning from life because God has a plan and purpose for every person he has created (Eph. 2:10). Christians and non-Christians alike share a lot of the same deep desires for love, security, worth, and meaning because God put those longings there. Those deep desires quietly point us back to the One who made us for himself. When you get people talking about the deepest desires of their hearts, God's Spirit can use that to show them important things. That's what this next exercise will do. This exercise will help you listen to the deepest longings and desires of the people you're getting to know. You will then reflect back and summarize what you hear. This has proven to often be a powerful, life-giving conversation for people who don't follow Christ, simply because no one has ever listened, taken such interest, and reflected back in affirming ways the deep desires of their hearts. Read Chapter 6 in *Unshockable Love* to see a real example of the impact Christina had by doing this exercise with her coworker (pp. 111-119).

How

- **Practice first.**

    The best way to prepare to guide a neighbor or coworker who has no faith through these questions is to first answer them yourself. You could even pair up in a group and practice asking and answering. Be particularly aware of your own feelings of vulnerability and what the person asking the questions could do to set you more at ease—discussing this will equip you to lead a powerful conversation with others.

- **Be straightforward.**

    The best way to broach the subject is to be straightforward. Tell your neighbor, coworker or friend: "I'm doing a personal growth exercise with my church (or group I'm in) to learn to better understand someone else's story and aspirations--to listen to the hopes and dreams of others. Would you be willing to let me hear your hopes and dreams?" Most people say, "Yes."

- **Be affirming.**

    For this to be a powerful experience for them, you must agree not to tell them what you think, share your story, preach, make judgments or react. You are, however, going to simply reflect back what you are hearing, affirming everything good that you can. Find a safe, comfortable place to meet—their home, a coffee shop, a scenic venue. Let them know it will take about thirty minutes to an hour (depending on how much they're enjoying it). Ask these questions and take notes, telling them you're going to feed back what you're hearing for their benefit.

- **Follow this outline.**
1. Ask, "What are your hopes and dreams in life?"

    The best way to focus may be to simply ask them what they want. Tell them, "Just fill in the blank, 'I want......' Try to come up with 20 or 30 things you want from life, and I'll help categorize what I hear."

    As they talk about what they want, or hope for, or dreams they have—encourage them to keep going and answer the question as many times as possible. Make notes and put numbers or symbols by similar "themed" statements. "I want to have a loving family…", "I want my life to make an impact on people…", "I want to be known for generosity" may all group together.

    Say back to them the main "themes" that emerge, and ask them if that accurately reflects what's most important or what they most want out of life. If they alter your summarized themes, don't argue or debate, just change them.

2. Take each of the main two or three desires and ask them, "Why?" Taking each one by one– "Why is this important to you?"

    This is a very important question because it drives to the deeper spiritual desires of our hearts— most people are not even aware of what drives their surface motivations and pursuits. Keep being curious about "Why." Ask why that matters so much in various ways. Because you are now delving into matters of the heart, be sensitive to encourage good motives and God-given desires. Don't say too much or get preachy—keep them talking, but affirm good motives where you can. Jot down words or ideas so that you can summarize back what you're hearing.

3. Make affirming observations.

    At this point, feed back to them what you've heard about their hopes and dreams. Summarize each of the main "themes," and the deeper reason or desire that you heard underneath. Ask them if that sounds accurate, or what they would alter. Tell them any encouraging, affirming words since they've probably gone deeper into their heart with you than they have with most people. Thank them for doing the exercise with you. If it seems appropriate, you may tell them, "You know, I'll be praying for _____ (that hope or dream) to be fulfilled—that's a God-honoring desire."

Act
I will ask _____ (name) or _____ (second person) to do this exercise by _____ (date).

Assess
- What surprised you most about the conversation?
- What did you learn about this person?
- How might God want you to follow up after your conversation?

Next (suggested exercises)
Listen for Their Spiritual Story
Telling Your Spiritual Story
Share the Good News

Speak the Truth in Love

Instead, speaking the truth in love, we will in all things grow up into him who is the Head, that is, Christ.
~ Ephesians 4:15

This exercise is based on the "Try This" activity in Chapter 5 on p. 103 in *Unshockable Love*.

> Let's be honest. Sometimes "speaking the truth in love" is just an excuse for telling others what we don't like about them, or why they are wrong and we are right. Jesus spoke the truth in love, but he did so in a way that others could not only hear the truth, but actually see that he loved them (Mark 10:21).
>
> Becoming like Jesus in this way is first about your ability to love. Unless someone is convinced that you love them and want only the very best for them, your truth is likely to be received as harmful rather than helpful. Even if you are certain about your love, you still need to be careful with your words. The same truth can be communicated in words that are accusing or in words that are affirming.
>
> The goal of this exercise is to practice speaking the truth in love in such a way that it is received as just that. Doing so is risky. If you want to help people become who God intended them to be, this is a skill you will need to master. Remember, the "truth" is not just about what's wrong, but also about the Masterpiece God sees and wants to restore.

How

You should approach this exercise with prayerful caution. This is not an opportunity to unload on someone you've wanted to confront. It is a challenge to share a truth with someone you care deeply about that will move them closer to Jesus. These tips will help:

- **Check your heart.**

  Before you have a conversation, take a few days to pray about the person and the issue. Ask for the Holy Spirit to reveal any judgment or hypocrisy in your heart. Ask him to show you the truth about what he intends for the person to become.

- **Check your truth.**

  The truth is not yours but God's. You need to be confident of that before you share it with someone else. Whatever the issue may be, get out your Bible and see what it says about it. Use a concordance or online Bible to search for relevant verses. These are not ammunition – just your certainty that this truth comes from God.

- **Consider your words.**

  Focus on the most affirming and encouraging way you can communicate this truth. Think about communicating hopeful truth along with challenging truth:

  1. What's the truth about the wonderful future God sees for this person?
  2. What needs to be addressed that might hinder that great future?
  3. Think seriously about how you personally believe God is going to do great things in and through your friend.

  Use these thoughts to sandwich challenging words between hopeful words. Speaking truth might not require corrective words, but spiritually challenging words for a person exploring faith. I remember saying to a guy, "What if it's true that God created you for himself and loves you more than any other person could—wouldn't you want to at least explore knowing that God?"

- **Speak gently.**

  Remember that your facial expressions and the tone of your voice will communicate as much or more than the words you say. Before you meet, consider how God sees this person as a dearly loved prodigal son or daughter and pray to communicate his love. Do your best to speak gently with a calm and quiet confidence. If you find the pace or volume of the conversation increases, it's a good indicator your message isn't being received in love and you should back off or back up and wait for another time.

Act

In the next _____ (time), I will meet with _____ (person) and seek permission to lovingly share the truth with them about _____.

Assess

- Were you able to have the conversation? How did it go?
- What did you learn about how to speak the truth in love?

Next (suggested exercises)

Share the Good News
A "Come as You Are" Invitation

Point the Way

*After Jesus had finished instructing his twelve disciples, he went on
from there to teach and preach in the towns of Galilee.*
~ Matthew 11:1

> Jesus came because God loved the whole world and wanted to make disciples of all people, but he spent most of his time with twelve men. From those twelve disciples, there are today billions of people who are following Jesus. It's tempting to focus on reaching the billions, but Jesus' way was to focus on training the few.
>
> That should be good news to you. Only a few people have the gifts needed to teach crowds of hundreds, much less thousands or more, but everyone can develop someone. As you build relational momentum, serve your neighbors, and have spiritual conversations, some of your friends will come to faith and choose to follow Jesus. As they do, you need to be ready to point the way.

How

Showing someone how to follow Jesus isn't as complicated or scary as it might sound. Here are some guidelines that will help you show a new follower the way.

- **Be intentional**

  Intentionality is the process of committing your will to a course of action. It's the difference between saying, "I should exercise," and actually going to the gym. Start by having a conversation about what you both want and what you are both willing to do.

- **Follow a plan**

  There is nothing wrong with having coffee with a friend once a week – and those kinds of relationships are often very powerful. Discipleship is more than that. There are many excellent resources to guide your spiritual growth. You may want to ask if there are resources your church recommends. *Unshockable Love* recommends some as well; you can find *Morph* and *Investigating the Way of Christ* at www.gatewayleaders.com.

- **Expect detours**

  Even with intentionality and a plan, expect detours. Children learning to walk fall down. New disciples get distracted, make mistakes, and even fall into temptation and old ways of sin. Be prepared to lovingly encourage them back onto the way of Christ.

- **Focus on the right goal**

    Jesus made disciples who made disciples. Keep this goal in focus. Learning the Bible is good, hearing and obeying the Holy Spirit is critical, overcoming sin is essential, but none of these things alone is the goal. From the very beginning, involve those you are leading spiritually in becoming followers of Jesus who help others follow Jesus.

Act

I will create intentional relationships with _____ (names) to help them become followers on the Way of Christ.

Assess

- What concerns or fears do you need to overcome as you enter into an intentional spiritual relationship with a new Christ-follower?
- How will you know if the relationship is producing spiritual fruit?

Next (suggested exercises)

Know How You Grow
Find a Running Partner
Growing Deep

Find a Running Partner

Therefore encourage one another and build each other up, just as in fact you are doing.
~ 1 Thessalonians 5:11

> Jesus shared life with his disciples. His disciples experienced life together with Jesus and each other, which probably explains why the rest of the New Testament is full of commands to encourage, help, love, and serve one another. These commands can easily become just good ideas that you don't really live out.
>
> Every Christian needs other Christ-followers to fully experience life the way God intended---a few people who are committed to encouraging one another on the Way of Christ. We call them spiritual running partners. Just like a friend who gets you out of bed to run, you need spiritual friendships to keep you pressing ahead in faith.

How

Running partners are two to four people in a similar spiritual season who agree to do life and faith together in total transparency. Here are some simple suggestions for getting started:

- **Find like-minded partners.**

  If your goal is to win a marathon, and your friend just wants to lose five pounds, running together may be more frustrating than fruitful. In the same way, spiritual running partners will be most fruitful if you share a season of spiritual life and at least a common direction. As you think of possible partners, share a copy of this exercise with them and ask if they would be interested.

  Note: Because of the "no secrets" nature of the running partner relationship, we strongly encourage all running partners to be of the same gender.

- **Follow the rules of running.**

  At your first get together, review these rules of running. Make sure everyone understands what they mean and is in full agreement with them. These rules are necessary to create the kind of trusting relationships where you can be totally transparent with one another.

  - Accept and give encouragement as often as possible.
  - Ask questions often; give advice only with permission.
  - Give reproof or correction only when absolutely necessary.
  - Never give judgment.
  - Always protect confidentiality.

The goal of running together is to become more like Jesus in your attitudes and actions. The purpose of your time together is not Bible study or prayer, though you will likely do those things together. The focus of your time together is to ask hard questions, determine what actions you need to take, and assess your progress. Use these questions to guide your conversations:

1. What do you think God is trying to do in your life right now?
   - How have you experienced the fruits of the Spirit lately (Gal. 5:22)?
   - How have you treated those you do life with?
   - What sin have you been conscious of this week?

2. If there's an area you need to focus on to better love God, love people, build character, or be Christ's Church, what would it be?

3. What's one thing you will intentionally do to take steps of growth?

4. Have you said the "last 10%" or have you held back today?

Act
I will meet _____ (frequency) with my spiritual running partner(s):

Assess
- What concerns or fears do you have about finding a spiritual running partner?
- What will be most difficult for you in keeping your running partner commitment? How will you overcome this?

Next (suggested exercises)
Know How You Grow
Growing Deep

Growing Deep

A student is not above his teacher, but everyone who is fully trained will be like his teacher.
~ Luke 6:40

> Jesus has a tendency to say things that are profound – simple to understand but hard to imagine. It's no real surprise that a student becomes like his teacher – until you see Jesus as the teacher and yourself as the student. Jesus is telling you that when you are fully trained you will be like him.
>
> Too often we see growth as knowing more about Jesus instead of becoming more like him. Knowing about him is safe, even comforting. Becoming like him is dangerous and daunting. It's not something you do on you own. It's something he does in and through you. It's where this journey began, with a question, are you like Jesus? If you've been doing these exercises, there are probably others around you now who also want to be like Jesus. Together you can be—as you grow deeply in him.

How

Growing deep isn't a single exercise. Growing deep happens as you put a number of exercises or activities into your life that will, in time, transform you to be like Jesus. These steps are not complete, but they will help you and those around you get on a path of growth.

- **Do this together.**

  This theme has repeated in many of these exercises. God designed you to grow together. Ideally, as a result of these exercises, you have some people around you who are ready to grow. Invite them to join you in growing together.

- **Determine the season.**

  Growth won't happen overnight, so make commitments to each other and the process with a long view. Don't fall into the trap of only learning and never teaching. From what we can tell, Jesus spent a full year training his disciples intently, then sent them out to do the same thing he was doing. In our experience, a year is an ideal season to commit to growth and equipping.

- **Decide on the goals.**

  One of the challenges of growing to be like Jesus is that it can become vague. Like a hike without a destination, your group can end up wandering through the wilderness. There are many good resources you can use to establish goals and guide your journey. We'd encourage you to explore the Morph experience described in *Unshockable Love*. Whatever you choose, make sure it's focused on helping you become like Jesus, not just know more about him.

- **Don't get discouraged.**

  If you've ever started a diet or exercise plan, you're familiar with how quickly your enthusiasm can vanish. Don't be surprised when the same thing happens with your spiritual growth. When someone falls behind, encourage them to get back in the game. When you hit a flat spot, and it doesn't feel like you're making any progress, lean in not out. When you experience conflict or confusion, commit to work through it together. All of these things are part of the process.

- **Celebrate the victories**

  If you commit to the process, God will do his work, and amazing transformation will happen in you and your group. Take time along the way to celebrate the growth you see in each other.

Act

We _____ (names) will grow together for the next _____ (time) in order to see each of us become more like Jesus.

Assess

- What concerns or fears do you need to overcome as you enter into a season of growing together?
- How will you know if your time together is producing spiritual fruit?

Know How You Grow

I planted the seed, Apollos watered it, but God made it grow. So neither he who plants nor he who waters is anything, but only God, who makes things grow.
~ 1 Corinthians 3:6-7

> Jesus spent three years preparing his disciples. The Gospels record much of what he taught them, but they also tell us they traveled together doing life as a group (Mark 8:27). After they had been trained for a while, Jesus sent them out to do the same things he did (Luke 9). All of these things prepared them in just three years to change the world.
>
> Here is an amazing thought—you can do the exact same thing! Jesus said, "All authority has been given to me," and "I am with you always." You can make disciples just like Jesus did.
>
> Here are two interesting questions: "What experiences have most helped you to follow Jesus?" "What experiences have most prepared you to be like him in attitude and actions?" These aren't just theoretical questions; they are very practical ones. Understanding how you and others have grown to become followers of Jesus will help you understand how you can help others grow too.

How

This exercise is something you can do individually as well as discuss as a group. Just follow these three steps:

- **Your personal growth experiences**

  Take some time to reflect on this question: What activities or experiences have had the greatest effect on your own spiritual growth? Journal your answers.

- **Others' growth stories**

  Individually or as a group, ask at least five people who are actively following Jesus the same question: "What activities or experiences have had the greatest effect on your spiritual growth?" Journal their answers.

- **Discover growth patterns**

  Individually or as a group, review what you learned about how people grow. Keep these two questions in mind:
  - What patterns do you see?
  - What are the implications of people's spiritual growth?

Act
I/we will complete the Know How You Grow exercise by _____ (date).

Assess
- What surprised you most about how people grow?
- What was most encouraging to you about how people grow?
- Whom will you invite to grow with you?

Next (suggested exercises)
Start a Group
Find a Running Partner
Growing Deep

Index

A "Come as You Are" Invitation	59
Be Available	7
Calling Out the Masterpiece	9
Check Your Connections	35
Create a Rhythm	39
Draw a Map	21
Find a Cause to Serve	45
Find a Running Partner	67
Go to the Hurting	47
Growing Deep	69
Have Fun with a Purpose	27
Have Powerful Conversations	61
Heart Storming	49
Invite Others	11
Know How You Grow	71
Know Your Gifts	17
Listen for Their Spiritual Story	53
Make a Covenant	19
Make a Meal that Matters	29
Make Room	37
Point the Way	65
Pray 4:4	23
Prayer Walk	13
Seeing Needs	15
Seeing Past the Mud	3
Serve Someone	41
Share the Good News	57
Speak the Truth in Love	63
Start a Group	33
Start Spiritual Conversations	51
Telling Your Spiritual Story	55
Throw a Party	31
Throw a Serve Party	43
Unshockable	5
Walk Don't Wave	25

About The Authors

Craig Whitney spent over 20 years in church ministry in roles that ranged from youth guy to church planter. He served for seven years as the Executive Director of Gateway Leadership Initiative. He lives in Roseville, CA with the cutest girl in his 4th grade Sunday School class in their almost empty nest. When he is not reading, writing or talking about mobilizing more leaders, he likes to spend time pedaling his road bike through the Sierra foothills.

You may also connect with him online at:
www.craiglwhitney.com
www.facebook.com/craiglwhitney
www.twitter.com/craiglwhitney

John Burke is the author of *No Perfect People Allowed*, *Soul Revolution* and most recently *Unshockable Love*. He is the lead pastor of Gateway Church in Austin, Texas, which he and his wife Kathy founded in 1998. Since then, Gateway has grown to over 4,500 members, made up of mostly unchurched people who began actively following Christ at Gateway. John is also the founder and president of Gateway Leadership Initiative (GLI), a nonprofit organization working to help church planting pastors and ordinary Christians "raise the church out of the culture." John has spoken in 15 countries to over 200,000 church leaders and Christians about reaching a postmodern, post-Christian culture. He and Kathy have been married twenty-five years and currently reside in Austin, Texas. They have two children, Ashley and Justin.

You may also connect with him online at:
www.johnburkeonline.com
www.facebook.com/j0hnburke
www.twitter.com/j0hnburke

Take The Next Step with *Unshockable Love*

So what's next?

How can I express the truth in this book through my life?

1 Go to **UnshockableLove.com**, where you will find resources that will help you implement the ideas from the book in your life, church, and small group:

- Network Action Guide
- Small Group Discussion Guide
- Church & Leader Resources

2 Go to **JohnBurkeOnline.com** for ongoing thoughts about living on mission with Jesus and each other.

3 Go to **GatewayLeaders.com** for more leadership training resources from John Burke.